T0352784

1972:
THE FUTURE
OF SEX

The Wardrobe Ensemble

1972: The Future of Sex was commissioned by Shoreditch Town Hall and supported by Arts Council England, Tobacco Factory Theatre's Artist Development Scheme and Bristol Ferment.

1972: The Future of Sex was first performed as a work-in-progress, formerly titled *The History of Fucking*, in October 2014 at Shoreditch Town Hall, and as part of Bristol Ferment at Bristol Old Vic in January 2015.

1972: The Future of Sex previewed at Latitude Festival and at Shoreditch Town Hall in July 2015 before premiering at ZOO Venues at the Edinburgh Festival Fringe in August 2015. The production was revived at Bristol Old Vic in May 2019.

1972:
THE FUTURE
OF SEX

The Wardrobe Ensemble

ORIGINAL CAST

RICH	Ben Vardy
CHRISTINE	Kerry Lovell
ANTON	James Newton
TESSA	Emily Greenslade
ANNA	Jesse Meadows
PENNY	Helena Middleton
MARTIN	Tom England

CREATIVES

Devised and written by	Tom Brennan, Tom Crosley-Thorne, Tom England, Emily Greenslade, Jesse Jones, Kerry Lovell, Jesse Meadows, Helena Middleton, James Newton, Ben Vardy and Edythe Woolley
Music	Tom Crosley-Thorne
Lyrics	Tom Crosley-Thorne and the company
Directors	Tom Brennan and Jesse Jones
Designer	Georgia Coleman
Lighting Designer	Rachael Duthie
Dramaturg	Edythe Woolley
Set Construction	Tom Crosley-Thorne, Rob Prentice and Cliff Thorne
Image	Louie Isaaman-Jones
Producer	Hannah Smith

Foreword by Rebecca Pollock

Rebecca Pollock is a screenwriter, lecturer and founding member of Shady Dolls Theatre Company

In 1995 when I was fourteen, I developed my first proper all-consuming musical obsession and, like so many before and after me, it was with The Beatles. My best friend Eleanor had been given a CD of the 1966 album, *Revolver*. We lay on her bed with all the lights out as the twanging opening chords of 'Taxman' started and at that moment something in my life irrevocably altered. I did not come from a family where music was played all that often, and certainly not music that sounded like this. Those thirty-five minutes and one second of splendour that we played on repeat for hours represented a complete and utter liberation. From that day, I spent the rest of my teenage years learning everything I could about the sixties and seventies. I imagined how it must have been to stroll down Carnaby Street in a sheepskin coat. I grew my hair long and wore flowered hairbands and flares, revelled in footage of sit-ins and protests and dismissed any talk of contemporary society with the knowing sneer of someone who understands there was once a better life. I fell deeply in love with the young Paul McCartney and practised kissing his picture on a life-size poster on my bedroom wall. I lay beneath it and lost hours fantasising about what it must have been like to be a student during the Wings university tour of 1972 where I may have actually had a chance of running into him in the student bar…

To culturally interested, educated millennials, sitting in the comfort of a more equal, economically stable and technologically advanced life, the allure of the sixties and seventies has never really faded. There is still great romanticism in the idea of Bowie stepping out on stage as Ziggy Stardust or the photos of the women shouting with rebellious pride as they protest at the Miss World pageant. We have a tendency to believe, as I did, in my Beatles-fuelled teenage haze, that it was unequivocally a more exciting, more dynamic time. That anyone who came of age in the sixties and early seventies must have surely been having a wild, uninhibited ride of free love, artistic experimentation and profoundly important political revolt.

But of course, that could never have really been the whole picture. England, for the most part, was still a country that prioritised tradition, old-fashioned family values, and a fairly broad sweep of political conservatism. 1972, the year of focus for The Wardrobe Ensemble, was actually a very special one. But it wasn't necessarily special because it was a particularly good year, or because of some of the more iconic moments of cultural history that it spawned. It was special because it marks a historical border between the 1960s – a decade that was indeed marked by idealism, experimentation and a certain degree of affluence – and the 1970s – a decade of conservative politics, unemployment, detrimental class clashes and escalating inflation. Looking back now, 1972, bridging this momentous 'before and after', appears on the history pages as a cacophony of confusion, contrasts and contradictions – a year of incredible social highs and lows. It is a period of twelve months that starts with Bloody Sunday and ends with the formation of the first Green political party. A period that produces the era-defining feminist magazine *Spare Rib*, but also *Playboy*'s highest-selling issue ever recorded. It was the year where, on stage, David Bowie's alter ego may have liberated and empowered isolated teenagers, but in the music studios and backstage of *Top of the Pops*, musicians and presenters were using their power and privilege to abuse that same generation. Twenty-three years later, my fourteen-year-old self may have looked to this time with longing, but in reality a teenage girl from a working/middle-class conservative family in Kent would have been twenty times less likely to attend university than her 1990s counterpart, let alone go on tour with Paul and Linda.

The Wardrobe Ensemble are only too aware of these nuances, and cleverly navigate how certain monumental moments of iconography and cultural resonance from 1972 offer compassionate insight into the very real struggles of everyday people dealing with their sexual identities and relationships. In the play, a family sits watching Ziggy Stardust emerge in all his glory on their one shared television set. The daughter rises out of her seat in triumph whilst her parents shrink and convulse in disgust as they promptly change the channel – there will be no watching it later on YouTube for her… In the hallowed halls of academia, a brilliant modern young woman gets turned on by her apparently feminist lecturer only to discover he is by no means interested in walking the walk he so passionately (for hours) likes to talk. And Anton – who likes to dress in his mum's clothes – struggles with having to confine his real identity to his bedroom.

Of course, the real brilliance of this show is that whilst we nod, smile and enjoy the historical references of music, time and place, we are really watching something that is just as much about ourselves as it is about the generations above us. A love letter to the sexual confusion and exploration of us *and* our parents, so to speak. It nudges us to consider that whether a Joni Mitchell or a Britney Spears concert, longing, fear, love and loss clash and collide throughout decades and across millennia. It is a show that you can watch with your friends, your parents and your siblings. A show that reminds you of the pain, pleasure and sometimes joy of sexual discovery, but also urges you to understand that no matter what era you come of age in, there will be social challenges, norms and conventions to confront.

In a year where our country is so uncertain of its future, where we are again in a twelve-year period that marks enormous change, *1972: The Future of Sex* has an even more profound impact as it makes us reflect on how nostalgia, and looking wistfully for an idea of when things were 'better', is misguided. Instead, the show encourages us to learn from the past; appreciate what it gave us, but use it to help us better understand and develop our present. Through great laughter and striking poignancy, the play lets us know that whilst generations may feel so greatly divided, we have all been, at one point or another, that teenager in their bedroom looking and wondering at their reflection in the mirror. And ultimately, when all is said and done, no matter what your musical or sexual preference, isn't that a wonderful and necessary reminder?

Rebecca Pollock, still a dedicated Paul McCartney fan
2019

A Note from Co-director Tom Brennan

'Mum, when did you first have sex?'

We began making this show under the working title *The History of Fucking* in the autumn of 2014 at Shoreditch Town Hall. We were feeling pretty uncomfortable about the state of sexual politics at the time and wanted to know how we had got to where we were. In those first two weeks, we made mountains of material. We researched, read, interviewed our parents (see above question), improvised, danced, played and talked. We talked about history, change, gender, identity, choice, equality, power, porn, love, sex, sex, sex. We talked about the inequalities present in our rehearsal room. We felt vulnerable and dangerous. We felt confused. When we first performed this show over the summer of 2015, I was surprised by a particular response. Often audience members who grew up in the 1970s talked to us after the show about how recognisable and real the world of the play felt to them. They would ask us:

'How did you know what X experience was like?' 'Was the story of Y real?'

And yes, we did a lot of research into the specific cultural landscape of early 1970s Britain to make it feel grounded. We made long lists of seventies' artefacts and cultural relics. But we were aware that the era is often depicted in either depressive social-realist hues; a vista of strikes, poverty and civil unrest, or as a psychedelic orgy of philosophising hippies and social rebellion. However, our conversations with our parents led us to find another reality: a generation of young people who (much like any other generation) felt like the party was happening in another room. Their desires were perhaps sparked by reading *The Female Eunuch* or seeing Bowie as Ziggy Stardust on *Top of the Pops*, but the vast majority of young people weren't about to join the revolution however much they wanted to. Instead they were trapped between the future and the past. They were trapped between a desire to become a gorgeous butterfly and the harsh reality of still living as a very awkward, very confused caterpillar. The reason I imagine audience members felt connected to the show, whether they had grown up in the 1970s or not, was that feeling painfully awkward and self-conscious about sex as a young person is a pretty universal human experience. I think another reason why audience members felt connected to the material is the spoken narration we used to build the world of the play. Words became a useful tool because of their ability to suggest rather than prescribe. Even though our word choices and rules of delivery were specific, the spoken narration was open to interpretation. It allowed audience members to fill in the blanks with their own lives. In the best cases, Christine watching a porno becomes you watching porn for the first time, Anna's first kiss with Tessa becomes your first snog on a scuzzy dance floor somewhere, Anton's bedroom becomes your bedroom. In the best cases, the set, the performers and the story all become conduits for your personal reflection. As Virginia Woolf said:

'Words do not live in dictionaries, they live in the mind... full of echoes, memories, associations, naturally. They've been out and about on people's lips – in the houses, in the streets, in the fields, for so many centuries... stored with other meanings, with other memories...'

And so, if you are interested in putting this play on in the future, I would encourage you not to overcomplicate any aspect of your production, nor to prescribe too heavily the emotional or intellectual meanings that you want the audience to receive. I would encourage you to allow space for the audience. Try not to judge. Even Brian. I'm proud that this show is open. Importantly, it is open to be read by a multitude of generations. And it is from this place of openness that we can acknowledge our collective confusion and begin to talk. It seems confusion is the only appropriate state to exist in when talking about sex. But as we continue to be confused, let's be as open, honest and welcoming about our confusion as possible. And in those rare moments when we have had the time and the space to talk, when we actually understand what is going on, let us be kind in our certainty. Peace and love, dudes.

Illustration by Laurie Stansfield

A Note from Musical Director and Composer Tom Crosley-Thorne

Music is integral to this play. Before *1972: The Future of Sex*, The Wardrobe Ensemble had always made their own music. But for the sound of the 1970s to be ingrained in the play, the group felt they needed to bring in someone external. As a gigging musician I came from a performing, songwriting and music-production background; composing in various styles for live bands, recording artists and short films, but this was my first production. I was brought into the first stage of the research and development process at Shoreditch Town Hall. During this time I was introduced to the devising process. It was a fast-paced room where anyone could write, perform or collaborate on anything. Things would get thrown at me, from Al Green to Ziggy Stardust, there was no time to be precious and at the end of each twenty-minute session you had to share. It was a fortnight of wah-wah guitar, space hoppers and glitter.

However, this process also brought up some challenges: What makes a song sexy? What is the sound of the seventies? How do I steer clear of pastiches or clichés? And how do I perform this music on my own? So I began by asking my parents what music they listened to in the seventies and what it meant to them. Out came their old vinyl collections consisting of James Brown, David Bowie, Earth, Wind, Fire, Mott the Hoople, Commodores, The Temptations, Parliament, to name a few… This music evoked a feeling of revolution. It is proud, fun and exciting. It is guitar, bass and drums. It is speaking for what you believe in and saying it simply.

It soon became clear to me just how much this iconic era changed the sound of music today. I was enticed by the simple instrumentation of the early funk records so decided that I would set myself the limitation of using only electric guitar, bass, keyboard and drums. It was very important to the group to have a musician onstage as it gave the show a particular live energy in having all of us make everything between us. So I performed lead guitar on top of backing tracks that were sequenced onto a loop pedal. The only music that I didn't compose is that of the late great David Bowie, as I wasn't going to do it justice. So there I was, with an electric guitar in one hand and a pedal board in the other, wearing bell bottom flares about to perform *1972: The Future of Sex* for the first time. I still hear my excitement in this music and I love listening to these tracks years later.

You can find the music at: www.soundcloud.com/1972thefutureofsex

Interview with the company, by Kate Wyver

Originally published 14 March 2016 in Exeunt Magazine

'We wanted to get the show to mirror the act of having sex,' says James (Jimmy) Newton, 'so it's build, build, build and then you reach a point where all the logic falls away.'

Interviewing nine people at once is more than a little intimidating, but as The Wardrobe Ensemble settle into the seats of the Tobacco Factory Theatre, they bubble with warmth and ease.

The company's latest show, *1972: The Future of Sex*, explores the awkwardness of three people's first time. Formed five years ago through the Bristol Old Vic's Young Company, The Wardrobe Ensemble have continued to grow, gaining critical acclaim and gathering a following in Bristol and beyond. Now they're going on tour with *1972*, starting here at the Tobacco Factory. It began with nine of them, and today has grown to include several more associate directors and musicians.

Jesse Meadows, one of the founding members, says 'We feel a deep rooting here because this is where most of us grew up and where we founded the company.' Although they are scattered all over the country now, most of their families are based in Bristol, so it'll always be home.

As we talk, they finish each other's sentences, especially when they all agree on a point. It's clear they've worked as a collective for a long time in how comfortable they are together, but being generous in letting each other speak is something they've battled with over the years. When they were performing their first show, *RIOT*, at the National Theatre Shed in 2013, Jimmy explains, 'we hit some real difficulties about the boy/girl balance in the room', and in how they were, Emily Greenslade adds, 'figuring out the best way of working as a group, all having strong voices at the same time.' Kerry Lovell explains that the balance of voices is still something they are hyper-aware of and that drawing on the frank conversations they had during riot helps to 'shape the room in a better way'. Jimmy adds, 'we've come a tremendously long way.'

Emily explains that *1972* arose from several conversations about sex. 'When we first started off we were going to make a show about Tom Brennan's (one of the company's directors) virginity,' she says. 'But then he lost it,' adds Jimmy, 'which was really annoying.' The idea was put on the back burner until Director Jesse Jones suddenly declared in the bar of the National Theatre that he wanted to make 'a play about fucking'. Jesse Meadows explains they spent time experimenting with ideas, including 'the idea of the history of fucking, the concept or whatever that meant, to see if it had legs'. After getting their brains whirring they did a two week R&D at Shoreditch Town Hall. This led to their first outing of *1972*, originally entitled – before awkward conversations with venue programmers and hesitant educational institutions – *The History of Fucking*.

Awkwardness around sex is a massive part of the show, which in part stems from lack of sex education in the seventies. Helena Middleton draws on the parallel with David Cameron's recent decision to stop compulsory sex education, 'We are going back to a time where sex education was ridiculous, but come on, it's still ridiculous now. We haven't made that many steps forward.' For the creation of the show the company members interviewed their parents, finding out how their sex education had been, as Tom England says, 'really misguided'. Since the seventies there has been an enormous shift in the way young people are exposed to sexuality. Ben Vardy says, 'there's this whole new wave of stuff that they've got to deal with, like dick pics and PornHub. We didn't have to deal with that. Shouldn't schools talk about all that?' Emily says their focus has been porn and hyper-sexualisation in the media, and how young people today are 'just being swamped with these images'. Jesse adds, 'it's not just about how you're taught about it at school, it's how people articulate it or discuss it in society.'

Exploring these ideas has been rewarding for the company members. Tom England notes the devising process has been 'really wholesome. It felt like the kind of things you should have spoken about when you were fifteen. It was so nice to hear that everybody thought about it differently, that everybody thought about sex, love, gender in different kinds of ways.'

1972 is the first show the company have toured with the original cast. Five years ago, over half of the company members hadn't started university yet, but now that they've all graduated there is more time to devote to The Wardrobe Ensemble. Kerry notes that in the last eighteen months they've been able to pay certain members of the company that they hadn't been able to before. But it's not yet a solid income for them all. 'We've all taken on all kinds of things,' she says, 'worked in supermarkets, libraries, pubs. We all individually, as practitioners and performers, take on other projects outside of the company all the time, which only serves to make the experience when we come back together even better.' Jimmy, himself a recent graduate, adds, 'we're still figuring out how to make it work best for us.'

As many smaller studio theatres in Bristol such as the Old Vic's Studio and the Brewery Theatre close their doors, while untraditional buildings such as the PRSC are opening their doors as theatres, we are entering an interesting time for theatre makers in this city. Jesse says the various reasons for closures of theatres 'makes a big difference of the landscape of theatre here' but what many of them note is the way theatres are speaking to each other a lot more, such as how Mayfest exists over many venues in the city. They agree that the changes happening in Bristol are making people incredibly resourceful.

When asked about projects in the pipeline they all look to producer Hannah Smith, unsure about what they are and aren't allowed to reveal. Having done a Christmas show for The Bike Shed for the past three years, this October the company is going to make a play on a farm with the help of city children. Jesse adds, 'We're continuing to tour this show in the autumn and tour other shows and expand the opportunities for those as well as making new things.' They are devoting four out of their eleven weeks on tour to doing R&D for new ideas and are currently having conversations with venues about different partnerships in the pipeline. They can't give away many details, but the Wardrobe Ensemble have plenty more ideas up their flared seventies' sleeves.

http://exeuntmagazine.com/features/wardrobe-ensemble/

A Note from Company Member Tom England

This article was first printed in the original programme for the show, August 2015

The Slow and Painful Dawn

As a teenager, the endless jostle for position amongst myself and others like me was a game framed by very base, often primal urges. The unspoken categories against which we judged ourselves and others were:

Who has 'got with' the most girls?
How many times have you had sex?
Is your girlfriend 'fit'?
Who is funniest?
Who is strongest?

The kindest, most caring and most intelligent of males rarely rose through the ranks unless they performed highly in one of the above categories. It's a game that I am thankfully no longer a part of. It has, nonetheless, left a mark. It consolidated a pattern of behaviour which is incredibly difficult to shake. It is not framed by thought, it is framed by power and privilege. It is, in my mind, a distinctly one-sided and grotesque game. It is shameful to participate in and yet I played it with a great deal of vigour. Not because I wanted to prove myself but because I had, by the age of thirteen, already grown so accustomed to drinking from the cup of male privilege that I found myself merrily dancing to the same tune my forefathers danced without question. In this game, women are subjugated and dehumanised. They are object and prize. They are no competition, they are other.

Let me be clear. I'm a nice man. I hope. I have nice parents. I am kind, considerate and friendly. But I have an asshole that lies within and the slow, painful dawning of that realisation is ongoing.

An example might help to convey what I'm trying to say.

I recall the searing jealousy I felt after hearing that my mate had 'got that girl naked on webcam last night', as he pointed at the fit girl everyone was leering at from afar at the County Athletics Championship, 2006. I didn't doubt it. His account fit neatly into the fantasy world I lived. The world in which I cruised MSN searching for girls from Redland to 'poke'. He had pointed out that she only agreed to expose herself after he promised he wouldn't tell anyone. 'As if he wouldn't tell his mates,' I thought.

That was me. I thought like that. I felt that way. I still do sometimes. I continue to inadvertently ogle at women, I continue to watch porn not because I want to but because I always have. I cannot fail to constantly be reminded of the position I occupy and the cup from which I drink.

Oh dear.

Many reading this will have the understandable response of 'Stop whining about the difficulties of being a man. Just stop it. Get over yourself and give the article room over to somebody who isn't moaning about the pain of being an inadvertent misogynist. Just stop being one!'

My response to those thinking that as they read is: Fair enough. Good point. Your thoughts are justified. But let me make one thing clear. I am writing this not to justify being an asshole but to publicly identify the exact shape and size of that asshole and to encourage others to do the same.

I guess my point is that the simple fact that women are fully human isn't something that men should learn when they pause to reflect. It should be obvious. It shouldn't be a truth that needs unravelling. It definitely shouldn't be something that you realise all of a sudden. It shouldn't be the case that young men are trained by the world around them to objectify, talk down to, and undermine. It is not just damaging to women, it is damaging to men too. It is upsetting, painful, and destabilising to slowly realise that you are performing as a man you no longer want to be.

It should be the case that all men see all women as fully human. It should be, and yet it isn't. How can it be when men like me think as one man and yet perform as another? It is embarrassing to admit you act in a way that compromises your imagined self. It is humiliating.

I don't know why I wrote this. It is an apology of sorts. An apology, not that I have any right to apologise on behalf of anyone other than myself, to women who have felt the ogling eyes and weight of male privilege bearing down upon them. It is also an admission of guilt and an expression of hope. Hope that future men won't feel this. Hope that the long and painful dawn is not only almost over for me, but for everyone. Forever.

I wrote that article in the summer of 2015 just after we had made *1972: The Future of Sex* and just before we took the show up to Edinburgh for the Festival Fringe. Since writing it a great deal has changed, both personally and politically. Scandals have unfolded. Movements have been born.

#MeToo
Weinstein
Trump
Spacey
R Kelly
Brock Turner
Many, many Women's Marches
etc., etc., etc., etc.

How depressing.

How hopeful.

Gender dynamics and gender politics have shifted. Things seem to have sped up since we wrote the show. Conversations have gained pace and traction. People are looking at how they speak and how they act with fresh eyes and some progress is being made.

It's been an interesting time to be a man. Since 2015 a giant mirror has been held up to the male experience and some very bright lights have been shone. Many are still wincing. Many are seeing things they never even knew existed. Including myself.

As such, reading the article I wrote in 2015 now feels strange. It feels strange because so often I find myself wondering if the best thing for me to do is to just, well, say nothing at all.

Stop making shows and writing things. Give over the space to someone different. That as a white, middle-class, straight, Christian artist, the most positive response would be to just give up the room. Stop making, saying and doing anything. Just shut up. Truthfully, I find it all a bit embarrassing that I even wrote an article entitled 'The Slow and Painful Dawn' about the difficulties of being a man. What a nause. Get a life. Stop it. Just stop.

And yet, I haven't.

I haven't stopped because the last few years have taught me, or perhaps shocked me, into pausing more, conceding more ground, asking for help. I'm learning to reconfigure, to move, act, and react in a different kind of way. I think other men are doing the same. I think that's more useful than doing nothing. I hope it is. There's still a way to go.

Illustration by Laurie Stansfield

A Note from Edythe Woolley, Dramaturg

In 1988, Prime Minister Margaret Thatcher introduced Section 28, legislation which banned the 'promotion' of homosexuality in schools and local authorities. This led to the closure of LGBTQI+ support centres and to the removal of LGBTQI+ issues from sex-education lessons. Any positive incentive or move towards embracing queer people in school was squashed and silenced. Section 28 remained in place until 2003 and we are still reeling from the impact it had on British culture today. For example, just a few weeks ago Conservative MP Andrea Leadsom said parents should be able to choose when their children are 'exposed' to LGBTQI+ issues in school and BBC *Question Time* debated whether it is 'morally right' for five-year-old children to be learning about LGBTQI+ issues. The fact that in 2019 a leading MP and national broadcasting network think it is okay to question the morality behind telling children that gay people exist and love each other just as straight people do is very concerning and points to how entrenched Britain is in its homophobic past. The resurgence of homophobia in the current government and media acts as a reminder that defending LGBTQI+ rights and supporting inclusive identity politics should not be seen as a thing of the past.

We 'Come Out.' We Come Out from the sea of heteronormativity declaring ourselves as non-heterosexuals. We step out of history's straight trajectory; deviating from the path that was set out by the generations before us. It is this deviation that offers the opportunity to find new routes and ways of being. Along these new lines we can create inclusive institutions, new structures of love and space for queerness.

This play was devised through our collective conversations around identity politics. We discussed our own sexualities, navigating difficult conversations about our desires, and how they have been influenced and misguided by dominant patriarchal culture, porn, movies, history and our legal systems. We grappled with the gender dynamics and power structures within our own rehearsal room and gave voice to personal experiences we hadn't shared before from shame and sexism to romance. We quizzed our parents on their sexual experiences during the 1970s and talked about the ways in which dating, with all its connotations, is different now. These difficult and sometimes taboo conversations felt integral to the creation of the play and we wanted our audience to feel like they too could have some of these discussions. So, when we first opened *1972: The Future of Sex* at London's Shoreditch Town Hall we launched a series of events that mirrored our personal and political learning celebrating the feminist and queer narratives that were at the forefront of our discussions.

For the duration of the run we installed a pop-up sex museum in Shoreditch Town Hall's basement. We created a timeline documenting the history of sex from 400 BCE to the present day, illustrated with images of ancient artifacts courtesy of Exeter University's Sex and History Project and with physical modern-day artefacts made and donated by artists and friends. The modern-day artefacts were creative and inspired. Donations included: cum-stained sheets and T-shirts from gay sex, bubblegum-pink home-baked 'fertility cakes', dildos on pedestals, drawings printed on knickers, huge inflatable beach balls with viscous liquid inside, lust poems, portraits of lovers and illustrations inspired by a fifteenth-century Arabic sex manual. All of the entries brought conversations surrounding sexuality, queerness and gender into focus. The artworks were visceral, bodily and emotional, exploding intimate and personal moments into the room. An interactive element of the museum further added to the personal collections; audience-goers were given the chance to include their sexual encounters on to the timeline. By the end of the run anonymous sexual experiences written on yellow sticky notes littered the historic timeline. Interrupting the chronology and spilling across white pages were new facts, personal histories, small revolutions, secret utterances; a collection of experiences that were expansive, joyous and timeless.

We also threw a 1970s-themed party in the venue's basement. Since then we have hosted two more of these parties, another at Shoreditch Town Hall and one at the Almeida Theatre. Across the events we programmed an array of queer cabaret and performance artists: Lady Vagina, a giant vulva, squirted cream onto pies, water-pistolled audiences and produced a red tongue of silk engulfing cheering crowds; drag king John Smith shaved his chest hair revealing his breasts whilst lip-syncing to a slowed version of Madonna's 'What It Feels Like for a Girl'; Kevin Le Grande, performance-artist-come-agony-aunt, was busy all night giving love advice to partygoers, who were donned in seventies' attire and glitter from our make-up station. DJs played until late. Wardrobe Ensemble cast members took over rooms as characters from seventies' movies, and wearing nothing but their underwear two members set up their musical instruments in a cupboard and delivered improvised love songs as a one-on-one performance. Drag queen Ellis D burst balloons posing as ballsacks; London's green queen Oozing Gloop sailed in on a tinfoil boat reciting the history of sex from the seventies to the present day; John Smith returned painting lipstick onto his bearded face and pulling eye make-up out from his underwear before creating a giant dress from bin liners, lip-synching all the while. Hula-hooping cabaret icon Symoné performed routines on roller blades; Lucy McCormick restaged biblical stories in the queerest way possible and one artist became an orgasming lampshade! These nights are about embracing the spaces in between. By following the lines of deviation we can leak, spill, and overflow from the structures of power that keep a repressive social order in place. When we stray from the straight lines of heteronormativity we create new structures, new modes of being and ways of loving freely.

We gather in a basement club, we sit together in a theatre, we pore over our lines, getting into character waiting for a shared applause. The Sultan of Brunei introduces a new penal code that punishes gay sex and adultery with death by stoning. Chechnya undergoes another anti-gay purge detaining and in some cases killing LGBTQI+ people. In the UK the Home Office is deporting queer people to countries where they face persecution at an unprecedented rate, denying 78% of queer asylum seekers in 2018. And London Pride feels more like a corporate party which has forgotten to address the shortcomings of our country's support for and acceptance of LGBTQI+ people. We should continue to celebrate, to be out and proud, but let's not forget that the first Pride was a protest and we still need to stand together for equal rights.

The Pop Sex Museum, artists and works:

Silence = Death, Artists in New York Fight Against Aids Rosa Van Praunheim (1989), *Pants To See my Mechanics* Laura Mallows, *Fertility Cake* Duncan Gibbs, *My Cum Stained T-shirt* Finn Love, *Mike and Tim* John Smith and Edythe Woolley, *Il Tricolore* Aidan Strudwick, *Lust Objects # 1, Lust Objects # 2, Lock Picked, Fuck Me* Clara Lipfert, *The Perfumed Garden of Sexual Delight* translations and illustrations by Lily Fletcher, *Balls* Alexandra Pitt, Will Seymour.

The Future of Sex: A Party, performers:

Amanda Hohenberg, Edythe Woolley, Ellis D, Especially For You, John Smith, Kevin Le Grande, Kheski Kobler, Lucy McCormick, Maxi More, Oozing Gloop, Symoné and The Wardrobe Ensemble.

1972: THE FUTURE OF SEX

The Wardrobe Ensemble

For our parents and our younger selves

Characters

ANTON
CHRISTINE
RICH
ANNA
TESSA
PENNY
MARTIN

The ensemble also play a range of other parts including:

PRESENTER
MUSICIAN/TOMMY
MICHAEL
MUM
DAD
TV PRESENTER
GEORGE
ACTIVIST
BRIAN
PORN ACTOR
ANTON'S DAD
LADY CHATTERLEY

Most of the time, narration in the show is delivered by the actors on microphones at the corners of the space.

The performance quality of narration is somewhere between the main character that they play in 1972 and the actors' present-day selves. There is a relationship between the narrator character and the onstage fictional character. We have used the performers' names from the 2015 run.

NARRATORS

ENGLAND (Tom England)
EMILY
KERRY
MEADOWS (Jesse Meadows)
HELENA
JIMMY (James Newton)
BEN

Note for Performance

Don't waste time with changing set pieces.
If a narrator says it's a pub, it is a pub.
Changes between scenes should be fluid and filmic.

Most stage directions refer to our production.
Future productions should feel free to play around.

(–) means an interruption.

(…) at the end of a speech means it trails off or it indicates
a pressure, expectation or desire to speak.

(/) means that the next character's text should start.

Song lyrics are in bold.

0.

A seventies' set.

Microphones in the corners.

A radio. Present-day pop songs playing. The lights dim and the radio quickly cycles back through time, playing clips of news, pop culture and songs until we arrive at 'All the Young Dudes' by Mott The Hoople from the year 1972.

A MUSICIAN *coolly enters, picks up the radio, eyes up the audience and saunters over to his guitar.*

The cast enter and sit on a row of chairs.

Finally, a final member of the cast, appearing as a PRESENTER, *enters and stands by a mic.*

1.

Music builds.

PRESENTER (*on mic, enthusiastic as hell*). This is it! For the first time this century, there are swathes of marriageable men. Britain might be a little under the weather. But the British people, especially the young, are grabbing life by the horns. Now is the time to p-p-pick up a boyfriend. This is the luckiest time to be alive and young. Sex is rampant and around every corner and the kids are grabbing it and grabbing it and saying yes! Yes! This is it!

Music cuts out. Harsh light on the cast sitting, silent and awkward.

Music builds again.

This! Is! It! The permissive society. The young are swinging, dancing and jiving. With a contraceptive pill in one hand and a tab of acid in the other, they enter the night. Casting away their morals into the dark and wolfing down that pill, they march on down the high street looking for unadulterated sex: Free sex! Free love! From a passing stranger. No young people have been so carefree, so loose, so blessed. Educated, rebellious and alive. These kids play it hard and fast, dancing like there is no tomorrow!

Music cuts out. The cast sit, even more self-conscious and awkward than before.

The music kicks in again as the PRESENTER *howls and throws themself across the stage.*

THIS IS IT! 1972! This! This! This! You are the children of the Age of Aquarius. Contraception was the key, and now you are free. Free-floating across the cosmos like groovy astronauts. Thousands of years have led up to this moment and this is it. A million colours spurt out of your mouth like some kind of crazy dragon. And your naked bodies collide in an infinity of everything. For this is what it means…

The PRESENTER *points at audience members.*

Love, Love, Love. You, You, You.

It's in your fate so grab it, grab it now!

The PRESENTER *turns to the rest of the cast, who look at him awkwardly.*

2.

ANTON*'s bedroom.*

ANTON, *a young-looking teenager, rises from his chair.*
A school bag is slung over his shoulder.

KERRY (*on mic*). This is Anthony. His parents call him
    Anthony. His friends call him Tony. He calls himself Anton.

ANTON walks into his room, sees himself in the mirror
and sighs.

He removes some sparkly, tight-fitting clothes from the bag
and lays them out on the floor.

He carefully takes out a record from his school bag. It is
David Bowie's Hunky Dory. *He hands the record to the*
MUSICIAN. *'Queen Bitch' plays.*

ANTON props the record sleeve up on a chair, goes back to
the mirror and sighs.

Angrily he removes his clothes, and stands in his underwear
examining his body, testing out different positions and
jiggling his tummy.

He puts his new clothes on, smiles, poses, likes what he sees.

3.

CHRISTINE*'s bedroom.*

CHRISTINE *and* RICH *enter and stand opposite each other,*
staring into each other's eyes.

JIMMY (*on mic*). Thursday 6th July 1972, 4:30 p.m. The walls
    of Christine's bedroom are covered in a repeating series of
    brown-hued hearts and circles, arranged into a pattern not
    dissimilar to tulips. A dog-eared print of David Cassidy
    hangs above her single bed. Rich tugs at the hem of her frilly
    white blouse, which used to be her favourite but lately she
    thinks may make her look like a tarty Smurf. They kiss.

CHRISTINE *and* RICH *move towards each other and kiss passionately.*

HELENA (*on mic*). They kiss as if there is nothing else in the world.

EMILY (*on mic*). Their two lips move softly against each other.

ENGLAND (*on mic*). Sharing spit and secrets.

JIMMY (*on mic*). They kiss.

ALL (*on mic, ad libbing. Not unison.*) And kiss. And kiss. And kiss. And kiss –

MEADOWS (*on mic*). Can we get on with this please?

JIMMY (*on mic*). A long kiss is a good kiss.

RICH *and* CHRISTINE *stop kissing.*

RICH. Babe, I've gotta split.

CHRISTINE. Nooo.

RICH. I have to. My soundcheck starts in like twenty minutes.

CHRISTINE. Can't they just do it without you?

RICH. Babe, I'm the frontman, they can't do anything without me.

CHRISTINE. Alright, bighead –

RICH. Oi! I'll see you at the gig, alright?

ENGLAND (*on mic*). Rich has only ever kissed three girls. The first was more of a peck on the lips, and it was when he was nine, and it was with his cousin Sally.

The second was with Angela, but she tasted a bit like gone-off milk.

But when Richard kissed Christine, it felt absolutely perfect...

CHRISTINE. Stay.

RICH. I can't.

CHRISTINE. Stay!

RICH. I can't, babe, / my soundcheck –

CHRISTINE. Rich. Stay…

RICH. You mean, stay stay?

JIMMY (*on mic*). She means sex.

EMILY (*on mic*). This is a big deal.

HELENA (*on mic*). Richard thinks Christine is the one.

ENGLAND (*on mic*). They first met when her best friend –

HELENA (*on mic*). – Michael –

> JIMMY *appears as* MICHAEL *in a leather jacket, as* RICH *disappears.*

JIMMY (*on mic*). – the drummer –

ENGLAND (*on mic*). – invited Christine to his gig.

> *Moments before a gig.*

MICHAEL (*on mic*). Christine! So glad you could make it. I think you're really gonna dig it.

CHRISTINE. Cool…

MICHAEL. One! Two! Three! Four!

> RICH *appears as the frontman of a funk/proto-punk band.* MICHAEL *mimes drums. Everyone dances.* CHRISTINE *is astounded.*

RICH (*singing into mic*).
Freaky Deaky girl,
Freaky Deaky girl,

ALL (*on mic, shouting*). **YEAH!**

> *Cut to after the gig.* MICHAEL *walks up to talk to* CHRISTINE, *but* RICH *cuts in.*

RICH. Hi, I'm Rich…

> RICH *moves to shake* CHRISTINE*'s hand. When their hands touch, they explode in slow motion.*

ENGLAND (*on mic*). And as skin met skin for the first time the internal elixir of love began to swash and swirl. Cheeks flushed, palms began to sweat. Dopamine met norepinephrine with a fizz pop bang.

CHRISTINE *and* RICH *begin to shake with increasing intensity until their bodies flop about on the floor.*

As the caudate nucleus lit up their primitive reptilian brains they became awash with oxytocin. 'Hold me' the reptile screamed, 'touch me'. Amorous endorphins plummeted, surged through these bubbling, bursting test tubes. Hands no longer hands, hearts no longer hearts, heads completely gone!

Back in CHRISTINE*'s bedroom.*

CHRISTINE. Rich. Stay…

RICH. You mean, stay stay?

JIMMY *and* ENGLAND (*on mic*). She means sex!

CHRISTINE. Tonight, after the gig.

RICH *screams with delight and high-fives a* NARRATOR.

RICH (*nonchalantly*). Yeah, I guess that sounds pretty cool.

CHRISTINE. Come round to mine. My parents are going to Norfolk.

RICH. I love… Norfolk.

CHRISTINE. I love Norfolk too.

They kiss passionately.

4.

A front room. CHRISTINE *and* RICH *transform into* MUM *and* DAD, *sitting in front of TV.*

Also onstage, ANNA*'s bedroom.* ANNA *stands checking out her skirt in the mirror.*

EMILY (*on mic*). Across town, a family is having dinner in front of the TV.

HELENA (*on mic*). Sausage casserole.

MUM. Angel Delight for afters!

ENGLAND (*on mic*). Photos of the three of them hang on the wall.

EMILY (*on mic*). Grandfather clock.

HELENA (*on mic*). The quiet tinkle of cutlery.

ENGLAND (*on mic*). Candles –

HELENA (*on mic*). Mum.

MUM. Mmm.

ENGLAND (*on mic*). Dad.

DAD. Mrmm.

EMILY (*on mic*). Anna.

MUM (*calling upstairs*). Anna?

DAD (*more sternly*). Anna?!

ANNA. Coming!

ANNA appears in the front room. She sits in front of the TV.

HELENA AS TV PRESENTER (*on mic*).…And now on *Top of the Pops*, we have Ziggy Stardust and the Spiders from Mars.

We hear the opening to Bowie's 'Starman'. ANNA rises out of her seat in enjoyment. MUM and DAD convulse in disgust.

DAD. He looks like Glenda Jackson dressed as Elizabeth I! Change the channel.

The sound of the channel changing.

ENGLAND AS TV PRESENTER (*on mic*). Fourteen Catholic civilians killed by British forces in Northern Ireland…

DAD. That's more like it!

MUM. You look nice.

EMILY (*on mic*). Anna is wearing the shortest skirt she has ever worn.

HELENA (*on mic*). Anna hopes this skirt will get her attention.

EMILY (*on mic*). Anna keeps a list of all the boys she has ever kissed in the back of her diary.

ANNA (*to* EMILY). You don't need to tell them that.

EMILY (*on mic, quiet*). Sorry…

ANNA (*to parents*). I'm going out.

MUM. Who with?

ANNA. Just some friends. This girl, Tessa.

HELENA (*on mic*). Five days earlier.

NARRATORS (*on mic*). Tessa!

HELENA (*on mic*). A slightly worn-down record shop
across town.

A record shop. TESSA *and* ANNA *are flicking through vinyl*.

ENGLAND *and* BEN *provide* TESSA *and* ANNA*'s inner
thoughts*.

ANNA *looks up at* TESSA.

ANNA'S HEAD (*on mic*). Look away look away look away
look away look away!

TESSA looks up. ANNA *looks down*. ANNA'S HEAD *gasps*.

She has lovely hair.

HELENA (*on mic*). Tessa does have nice hair. Not because she
spends lots of time caring for it, but because it naturally sits
on her head in an interesting way.

KERRY (*on mic*). A sort of cross between Carole King and
Janis Joplin. Tessa is wearing suede lace-up boots and got up
extra-early to put them on. She once got out of going to bed
with a man, by saying…

TESSA *turns to the audience*.

TESSA. It would take too long to undo my boots.

KERRY (*on mic*). Anna cannot see these boots due to the large
record collection in front of her.

HELENA (*on mic*). But don't worry, she'll see them later.

ANNA'S HEAD (*on mic*). Ask her a question, ask her a question,
just think of a question and ask her.

TESSA *picks up a record.*

ANNA. You got that?

ANNA'S HEAD (*on mic*). Course she hasn't got that, why would she be looking at it if she had it?

ANNA. – I've got that. It's just a recommendation really. I would recommend it. From me. To you. It's just a recommendation.

ANNA'S HEAD (*on mic*). – Stop saying recommendation.

TESSA'S HEAD (*on mic*). Maybe I should ask her a question…?

TESSA. So you're a Bowie fan then?

TESSA'S HEAD (*on mic, working it out*). Bough-we? Bow-we? Boo-we?

ANNA. Erm.

ANNA'S HEAD. I know literally nothing about the man.

ANNA. Really big fan, yeah.

ANNA'S HEAD (*on mic*). What are you doing?

TESSA. Cool! What's your favourite album?

ANNA'S HEAD (*on mic*). Fuckfuckfuckfuckshitshitfuckfuck –

ANNA. Greatest Hits!

ANNA'S HEAD (*on mic*). Nailed it.

TESSA. Right.

TESSA'S HEAD (*on mic, laughing*). 'Greatest Hits'?! I guess she is kind of cute when she lies.

KERRY (*on mic*). At precisely the same moment, their eyes meet across the vinyl.

ANNA *and* TESSA *look into each other's eyes.*

ANNA'S HEAD (*on mic*). Why is she looking at me like that? She is so beautiful!

An ACTIVIST *appears with loudhailer. Sound of crowds.* TESSA *and* ANNA *stay still, looking at each other.*

ACTIVIST. EVERYONE HAS A RIGHT TO LOVE.

HELENA (*on mic*). Meanwhile, central London. Seven hundred people. For the first time in British history.

ACTIVIST. THE GAY LIBERATION FRONT WILL NOT BE SILENT!

KERRY (*on mic*). Tessa pushes her hair behind her ear.

ANNA'S HEAD (*on mic*). Why can't I stop looking at her?

KERRY (*on mic*). Anna gulps.

ANNA'S HEAD (*on mic*). What does she want from me?

HELENA (*on mic*). They gather by the lions in Trafalgar Square.

ACTIVIST. WE WILL NOT BE INVISIBLE!

HELENA (*on mic*). And they let themselves be known.

ACTIVIST. WE WILL NOT BE ASHAMED!

HELENA (*on mic*). Despite the police lining up, their truncheons in hand, the people kiss.

KERRY (*on mic*). From across the record store, over the vinyl labelled A to J, Tessa and Anna *really* look at each other.

ANNA'S HEAD (*on mic*). She can't look at me like that. Why is she looking at me like that?

KERRY (*on mic*). Tessa and Anna really look –

HELENA (*on mic*). In the middle of the street, in broad daylight, the protesters kiss.

ACTIVIST. WE WILL BE FREE!

The ACTIVIST *disappears*.

KERRY (*on mic*). And Tessa says:

TESSA. So.

ANNA. So.

TESSA. Are you up to anything on Thursday night?

ANNA'S HEAD (*on mic*). Sitting at home watching TV with my parents.

ANNA. Just hanging out.

ANNA'S HEAD (*on mic*). – with my parents.

TESSA. There's a few of us going to Cross Club down the road. Wanna come?

ANNA'S HEAD (*on mic*). The Cross Club? Yes, more than anything in the world.

ANNA. Yeah cool, man. Chilled.

TESSA. Cool. Eight o'clock. Ask for Tessa.

NARRATORS (*on mic*).TESSA TESSA TESSA TESSA TESSA.

We return to ANNA*'s house.* MUM *and* ANNA *sit on the sofa looking up at* ANNA'S HEAD, *who is chanting.*

ANNA'S HEAD (*on mic*). TESSA TESSA TESSA TESSA.

MUM. Darling?

ANNA'S HEAD (*on mic*). Sorry.

ANNA'S HEAD *changes back into* DAD *and sits back into his place in the front room.*

DAD. Just make sure you're back by ten.

MUM. Let's say eleven.

DAD. Alright. Give us a chance to play that new board game I bought. I think it's called *Risk*…

DAD *mumbles as* MUM *screams a giant silent scream. At the same moment,* EMILY *becomes* MUM'S HEAD.

MUM'S HEAD (*on mic*). *I HAVEN'T HAD SEX FOR FIFTEEN YEARS!!*

MUM *snaps back to sitting quietly in the front room.*

DAD. The trick is to capture Australia first…

MUM *grabs* ANNA *and drags her up from the sofa and out of the front room.*

MUM'S HEAD (*on mic*). *GET OUT! GET OUT! LIVE YOUR LIFE WHILE YOU STILL CAN!*

5.

A pub.

MEADOWS (*on mic*). A pub. Music.

> *Loud rock music plays.*

> Soft music.

> *The loud rock music is replaced by a relaxed bluesy tune.*

> The pub is busy.

> *The* NARRATORS *create pub-hubbub.*

> Martin, a lecturer in English –

> MARTIN *enters.*

MARTIN. Sociology.

MEADOWS (*on mic*). – is sitting alone.

> MARTIN *sits.*

> Penny, his student –

> PENNY *enters and sees* MARTIN.

> …notices him from across the room. Her heart rate rises from seventy beats per minute to one hundred and ten.

> *Pause.*

MARTIN. Penny.

MEADOWS (*on mic*). That morning.

> *A university seminar room. Students chat excitedly.*
> PENNY *sits in the middle of a line of students. She stares at*
> MARTIN, *who stands at the front of the class.* GEORGE,
> *a student, whistles Donny Osmond's 'Puppy Love'.*

> A seminar room. The faint scent of hairspray and sweat on polyester.

MARTIN. Good morning… settle down, was that you whistling 'Puppy Love', George?

GEORGE. Sorry, sir.

MARTIN. Let me just make one thing very clear, stop whistling Donny Osmond or you'll never step foot in my lecture room again, thank you.

This morning we are going to return to our analysis of Greer's controversial *The Female Eunuch* with an eye to compare it with Anne Oakley's not-quite-so controversial *Sex, Gender and Society*, asking ourselves the questions: which is more empowering to the cause of female liberation and, in which of these futures, if either, would you rather live?

MEADOWS (*on mic*). When Martin taught his seminars, Penny felt like her whole world was shifting.

A fantasy. Everything slows down. PENNY *can't take her eyes off* MARTIN. *Her* CLASSMATES *dance. The sequence should be full of sincere, abstracted eroticism.*

(*Building to a climax*.) 1792: Mary Wollstonecraft published *A Vindication for the Rights of Woman*. 1850: campaign for improved female rights in employment and education. 1858: first British feminist periodical. 1876: universities open to women. 1908: two hundred and fifty thousand people gather in Hyde Park in support of women's suffrage. Votes for Women! 1913: Emily Davison died under the King's horse. 1928: women over twenty-one got the vote. Kinsey. Masters and Johnson. 1961: The pill. 1963: *The Feminine Mystique*. 1967: abortion became legal. 1968: women strike in Dagenham. 1970: protest at Miss World. *The Female Eunuch*. Equal pay. 1972: *Spare Rib*. – The world has opened up for women!

We return to the pub.

MARTIN. Penny.

Pub noise returns.

What are you doing here? / Silly question.

PENNY. Just having a drink with some friends.

Pause.

Who are you here with?

MARTIN. Just killing some time before catching a film.

PENNY. Which film?

MARTIN. *Cabaret*.

PENNY. Fab. I saw it yesterday.

   PENNY *pulls up a seat and sits next to* MARTIN.

MARTIN. Yeah – that's why I'm going. When you mentioned it earlier it sounded fantastic.

MEADOWS (*on mic*). One hundred and twenty beats per minute.

PENNY. You are going to find it so interesting. It's completely related to what we've been talking about in class. There's this bit…

MARTIN. Don't give it away.

PENNY. But even the way she looks is fascinating. She's got this short hair and she's so sexy and even though she's using her body and voice to get money, she's in control, she's the powerful one. So then the pregnancy…

MARTIN. Whoa.

PENNY. Sorry. I said nothing.

   Pause.

   I took your advice by the way.

MARTIN. Ah, the Union position?

PENNY. Yeah, I'm running for President actually.

MARTIN. Wow, that's fantastic. I'm glad you decided to go for it.

PENNY. Well I wouldn't have gone for it unless you had suggested it.

MARTIN. Well I wouldn't have suggested it unless I thought you could do it.

PENNY. I have to give a speech though. I'm not used to speaking in front of that many people.

MARTIN. You're speaking fine just now. Just imagine that you're talking to me.

PENNY. Okay… Anyway, enjoy the film.

MEADOWS (*on mic*). She goes to leave.

PENNY *doesn't rise from her seat.* PENNY *and* MARTIN *hold eye contact.*

She goes to leave…

PENNY *doesn't move.*

(*A little peeved.*) Penny goes to…

PENNY *suddenly rises from her seat and starts to leave.*

MARTIN. Penny?

PENNY *stops and turns.*

What would you say to seeing the film again… with… me?

PENNY *returns to her seat.*

6.

CHRISTINE *enters.*

JIMMY. Christine is thinking about tonight, after the gig.

Christine is thinking about Rich.

Christine is thinking about sex.

Christine is thinking about sex, with Rich, tonight, after the gig.

She recalls everything she has ever heard about sex.

Everyone enters and makes abstracted, rhythmic moves, panting and thrusting. This sequence should be fast-paced, full of energy and music. One at a time, they apprehend CHRISTINE *with their advice.*

MEADOWS. You don't want to get it wrong. You've only got one shot.

RICH *appears above everyone in flashback for a moment.*

RICH (*on mic*). I LOVE NORFOLK!

ENGLAND. It's certainly a messy business. Sticky.

HELENA. Don't be like Brenda.

CHRISTINE. Who's Brenda?

JIMMY. If you get it in your eye, it will blind you, and you might die.

EMILY. If you swallow it you will become pregnant immediately.

JIMMY. The devil enters through the heart and out of the penis, yeah!

ENGLAND. A man fell asleep in a woman and turned into a ball.

HELENA. You don't want to make an abortion out of it.

EMILY. Just ask your mum!

HELENA. Or your GP.

BEN. Or you could ask –

MICHAEL enters.

CHRISTINE. Michael!

Everyone else disappears.

MICHAEL. Christine! So good to see you.

CHRISTINE. Shouldn't you be at the soundcheck?

MICHAEL. Soundcheck… Nah, I don't have to be there for another hour or so.

CHRISTINE. Really?

EMILY (*on mic*). Christine never had a brother, but Michael and Christine have known each other since they were three.

BEN (*on mic*). Their fathers met at a skittles match in 1958 and the families have been very firm friends ever since.

ENGLAND (*on mic*). When they were nine, he sent her an anonymous Valentine's card… in March.

HELENA (*on mic*). When they were thirteen Christine joined the athletics club and Michael signed up the following week, even though he had asthma.

EMILY (*on mic*). When they were fifteen –

MEADOWS (*on mic*). Yeah we get it, he likes her. Now, they're on Brewer Street in the centre of town.

CHRISTINE. I think I'm going to do it.

MICHAEL. What, with Rich?

CHRISTINE. Yeah.

MICHAEL. When?

CHRISTINE. Tonight.

MICHAEL. Well that's really soon.

CHRISTINE. Yeah.

MICHAEL. That's *really* soon.

CHRISTINE. Yeah.

MICHAEL. You're ready then?

CHRISTINE. Yeah… No… I mean, I don't know. I'm a bit nervous…

MICHAEL. I think you should postpone.

CHRISTINE. What?

MICHAEL. I think you should postpone.

CHRISTINE. Why?

MICHAEL. Even if it's just for a tiny little while. Christine, this is a huge decision, this is the BIGGEST decision that you will ever have to make in your life. – And I just want it to be special for you, because you're special. I know you so well –

CHRISTINE. Yeah you're my best mate.

MICHAEL. YES! And you're my best friend. And I know you and I know how cool you are and how chilled you are and what a groovy cat you are, and I dig all that, really. Plus the mechanics are really tricky. You have to know what goes where, and when, and for how long. So I just think if you put it off for just a little while then maybe I can help you. I can teach you…

CHRISTINE. Michael? What are you doing?

He moves forward and leans in for a kiss. She pushes him away.

Whoa! Not cool.

Silence. MEADOWS *enters and smacks* MICHAEL *several times with a space hopper.*

EMILY (*on mic*). Michael and Christine will not speak again until their late twenties.

…Michael leaves.

MICHAEL *leaves, shell-shocked.* CHRISTINE *stands central, facing out front.*

With his words still ringing in her ears, Christine turns and looks up. She's in front of Vinny's Adult Video Store. She looks at the advert in the window. 'Private Screening. Rated X.'

BEN (*on mic*). A digression. It might be important to recognise that the second most common Palaeolithic cave painting depicts people with exaggerated sexual characteristics. Giant penises, globe-like breasts.

It seems with every new visual medium since, from the Papyrus to the Polaroid, pornography quickly follows.

Photography 1839, nude photography 1840.

In 1972, the adult film *Deep Throat* will smash box-office records to become the most profitable independent film of all time.

In 2014, one website, Pornhub, will receive seventy-eight-point-six billion views in one year, that's over eleven videos for every human being on earth.

In 2015 –

HELENA *raises her hand and* BEN *stops talking.*

HELENA (*not on mic. Looking at* CHRISTINE). In 2015, Christine's daughter writes in her diary:

'Yesterday my boyfriend told me he watches porn. It makes me feel uncomfortable but I can't articulate why exactly. I don't think it's because his expectation of sex was based on the years of porn he watched before he'd even kissed a girl. I don't think it's because he wants me to do the things women do in porn, I can say no. I think it might be because he has sex in reality, and yet he continues to watch the fake version, although he insists he only watches home videos. All I can say with any certainty is that it makes me feel uneasy.'

EMILY (*on mic*). But right now, in 1972, Christine looks up at Vinny's Vids and walks inside.

CHRISTINE *leaves*.

7.

MEADOWS (*on mic*). The pub.

The NARRATORS *create background chit-chat.*

JIMMY. Last orders!

NARRATORS (*on mic*). Two Blue Nuns please! Lager shandy, mate! (*Etc., etc.*)

MEADOWS (*on mic*). Penny and Martin have missed the film. They have spoken about...

JIMMY (*on mic*). Jane Fonda,

EMILY (*on mic*). fondue,

KERRY (*on mic*). the fact that Martin can't swim,

MEADOWS (*on mic*). their parents,

BEN (*on mic*). their pets,

EMILY (*on mic*). their pet peeves,

KERRY (*on mic*). Vietnam,

MEADOWS (*on mic*). space hoppers,

JIMMY (*on mic*). VHS,

BEN (*on mic*). Betamax,

JIMMY (*on mic*). – Wasn't invented yet.

BEN (*on mic*). Oh.

EMILY (*on mic*). Simone de Beauvoir,

KERRY (*on mic*). Women's liberation,

EMILY (*on mic*). Books,

BEN (*on mic*). Books,

MEADOWS (*on mic*). Books…

> MEADOWS *puts a book into* PENNY's *hands.*

PENNY. This is the bit I wanted to talk to you about:

> 'She lay quite still, in a sort of sleep, in a sort of dream.
> Then she quivered as she felt his hand groping softly, yet
> with queer thwarted clumsiness, among her clothing. Yet the
> hand knew, too, how to unclothe her where it wanted.'

> You see the hand has more agency than the woman does!

MARTIN. Which is interesting because she wants it as much as
he does.

PENNY. Exactly. Because she's sexually repressed and yet
Lawrence can't just write that it's the woman who wants to
have sex.

MARTIN. It's potentially to do with the time it was written.

PENNY. It was published in 1960.

MARTIN. But written in 1925.

JIMMY/KERRY (*on mic*). '28.

MARTIN. '28.

PENNY. Oh. So, it goes on to say:

> *The* NARRATORS *begin a sensual soundscape as* MARTIN
> *melts in his seat and onto the floor.*

'He drew down the thin silk sheath, slowly, carefully, right down and over her feet. Then with a quiver of exquisite pleasure he touched the warm soft body, and touched her navel for a moment in a kiss. And he had to come in to her at once, to enter the peace on earth of her soft, quiescent body. It was the moment of pure peace for him, the entry into the body of the woman.'

MARTIN *reforms himself and touches* PENNY*'s hand with his own.*

MARTIN (*quietly*). Penny…

GEORGE *enters carrying a petition and whistling 'Puppy Love'. He sees* MARTIN.

GEORGE. Hello, sir! Perhaps you'd be interested in reading and signing this?

He hands MARTIN *the petition.* GEORGE *directs everything he has to say at* MARTIN.

MARTIN. Hello, George, bit late to be campaigning, isn't it?

GEORGE. It's just that I'm sending the signatures off in the morning. Nixon is teetering on the edge so we need to keep voicing our opposition to this war.

MARTIN (*signing the petition*). Apparently it won't be long before he pulls the ground troops.

GEORGE. Absolutely. Well, let's turn that rumour into a reality and get the planes out to boot!

GEORGE *sees* PENNY.

Sorry, I hope I wasn't interrupting anything.

MARTIN….No, we were just chatting actually, George.

GEORGE. Sure.

GEORGE *goes to leave.*

MARTIN. George, don't you want Penny to sign?

GEORGE. Of course.

GEORGE *hands* PENNY *the petition. She signs.* GEORGE *looks at* MARTIN *knowingly.*

GEORGE (*to* PENNY). Aren't you the one running for the Union President position?

PENNY. Yeah.

GEORGE. That's great, so ambitious. Well done you.

GEORGE *leaves. A silence.*

PENNY. What are you reading at the moment?

MARTIN. I'm actually not reading anything at the moment. I'm writing.

Poetry. Poems.

PENNY. Oh. I'd love to read them.

MARTIN. Yeah. I'd love for you to read them some time too.

MEADOWS (*on mic*). He goes to leave.

MARTIN *rises from his seat and starts to leave. He stops, sighs and turns back.*

MARTIN. They're actually in my flat. It'll take me five minutes in the Cortina.

I could grab them and come back.

JIMMY (*on mic, more stern*). He goes to leave.

MARTIN *turns to leave again.*

PENNY. No, don't do that. It's silly to make two journeys. I'll come with you.

KERRY (*on mic*). Martin goes to –

MARTIN. Yeah, okay. Let's go.

8.

ANTON*'s bedroom*. ANTON *stands, tense. He pushes his hair behind his ear.*

KERRY (*on mic*). This is Anthony. His parents call him Anthony. His friends call him Tony. He calls himself Anton.

Loud funky music. ANTON *opens a make-up bag and pulls out red lipstick, which he liberally applies.*

He then pulls out a tub of glitter and applies it to his cheeks.

He poses confidently.

NARRATORS (*singing*).
He was looking down a kaleidoscope.
Stars were shining, giving me hope
Things were flying, we've been here before.
Gotta play the game
Gotta play the game
Or you'll lose the score

Gotta run, gotta run, gotta run,
Here they come, here they come, here they come,
Gotta run, gotta run, gotta run...

ANTON *takes the record sleeve and holds it up above his face.*

He dances.

He flirts with the record sleeve and kisses it.

Now we're sinking, into our candy-floss dreams,
Walls are closing, on our cigarette rings,
Judy's laughing, we've been here before.

Please shake my hand, Mr Starman
Please shake my hand, Mr Starman

ANTON *places the record sleeve on a chair, circles it, then struts towards it.*

He kneels down and starts to masturbate.

Gotta run, gotta run, gotta run,
Here they come, here they come, here they come,
Gotta run, gotta run, gotta run...

9.

A disco. No music. TESSA *and* BRIAN *dance in slow motion.*

Until the music starts, TESSA, BRIAN *and* ANNA *should do the moves that* BEN *suggests.*

BEN (*on mic*). Tessa is dancing with Brian.
Brian is an eighteen-year-old rugby player from Rugby.
Eight o'clock.

ANNA *enters, looks around.*

Anna.
The club.
The air is thick with sweat and cigarette smoke.
People.
Many, many people.
Where is she?

ANNA *sees* TESSA.

Tessa is dancing with Brian.
Tessa and Anna see each other from across the room.
Tessa moves away from Brian.

BRIAN *continues to dance unchanged.*

Tessa moves closer to Anna.
They dance.
Brian is confused.

BRIAN *turns, and looks confused.*

They dance.

Loud disco music, dance sequence.

Suddenly everyone in the club dances around TESSA *and* ANNA.

ANNA. Did you see Bowie on the TV?

TESSA. Yeah it was amazing.

ANNA. When he put his arm around the guitarist!

TESSA. Awesome!

ANNA. My dad freaked out.

TESSA. You still live with your parents?

ANNA (*looking for a way out of the crowd*). Er. Do you want
a drink?

TESSA *grabs* ANNA*'s arm as everyone melts away.*

TESSA/TESSA'S HEAD (*whispering in* ANNA*'s ear*). You're
beautiful.

TESSA *kisses* ANNA.

Fantasy.

David Bowie's 'Starman' plays.

The stage fills with light. ANNA *is lifted up and floats off
into the cosmos.*

Planets circle her.

She floats back down to the disco.

Everyone is looking at them. TESSA *and* ANNA *look
around uncomfortably.*

TESSA. Come on.

TESSA *grabs* ANNA *and pulls her away.*

The party dissipates, leaving BRIAN *alone. He dances in
silence.*

BEN (*on mic*). Brian is confused.

Brian is very confused.

This confusion will turn to anger. In 1982 Brian will attend
a Gay Pride parade, follow a man home, punch him in the
jaw seven times, drag him to the floor and kick him in the
stomach three times, rupturing his spleen.

But right now, in 1972, Brian is confused.

Brian is very confused.

10.

CHRISTINE *sits in the cinema.*

Sounds of a porno. Two MEN *sit down on either side of her.*

She takes out a notebook and starts to take notes.

RICH AS PORN ACTOR (*on mic, American, slow, deep*).
I understand what seems to be the problem. Your clitoris is located in the back of your throat.

CHRISTINE. It is?

RICH AS PORN ACTOR (*on mic*). It's okay, it's better than having no clitoris at all. You just need to learn to relax the muscles in the back of your throat.

CHRISTINE. Okay.

RICH AS PORN ACTOR (*on mic*). Just relax.

CHRISTINE. Like this?

The MEN *in the cinema slowly stretch open their mouths.*

CHRISTINE *slowly opens her mouth until it is wide open.*

RICH AS PORN ACTOR (*on mic*). That feels so good. That feels amazing.

11.

This sequence should be like a film montage, images (real, abstract or otherwise) weaving in and out of each other. Energetic music.

A street.

EMILY (*on mic*). Christine leaves. She bursts through the doors of Vinny's Vids and into the night.

Her legs are moving fast but she can hardly feel them hit the floor. Her reflection repeated in every windscreen and shop window. A kaleidoscopic image split into hundreds of pieces.

In another part of the stage, moments before RICH*'s gig.*

RICH. Michael, where's Christine?

MICHAEL. I don't know, we need to start.

RICH. I'm not starting the gig without her, I wrote this first song for her.

MICHAEL. Forget about Christine…

RICH *starts retching.*

What's wrong with you?

The focus shifts back to CHRISTINE *on the street.*

EMILY (*on mic*). She keeps moving. Eyes appear from nowhere and scan the details of her body. Her skin through her frilly white blouse. She imagines David Cassidy floating down from the poster above her bed and he's stopped kissing and started fucking.

Back to the gig.

MICHAEL. Are you gonna be sick?

RICH. I just get queasy when I'm worried about her, mate, I'll be fine.

MICHAEL. Rich, me and Tommy are waiting for you. Get on that stage and sing, now.

MUSICIAN AS TOMMY. Come on, mate!

MICHAEL. One! Two! Three! Four!

RICH. Fine.

RICH *runs up to a mic. During his singing, we see* CHRISTINE *running and a kaleidoscopic vision appear before her: men who are also running. They stare, smile, lick their lips and wink, before disappearing.*

(*Singing.*)
Oh,
You were my Freaky Deaky Girl,
You rocked my whole entire world,

And I'd do anything for you
You're the one on the run with your bright-blue eyes,
Take my hand and we'll fly! Yeah…

PENNY *and* MARTIN *appear in the Cortina.*

MEADOWS (*on mic*). Penny and Martin. Inside his Ford Cortina. The back of Penny's legs stick to the black-leather passenger seat. Her eyes rest on the hard polished-pine steering wheel as Martin's hands move from ten to two, to twelve to one, to half-past midnight.

KERRY (*on mic*). They're turning left.

TESSA *runs in closely followed by* ANNA.

TESSA. Come on!

ANNA. I can't believe you didn't pay for those chips! You're so bad.

TESSA. Chill out.

ANNA. I don't want to be an accomplice!

TESSA. Too late for that!

They climb a wall and walk across it.

ANNA. It's too high.

TESSA. Come on, you can do it!

ANNA. Alright, watch this!

TESSA *and* ANNA *jump off the wall. We see* CHRISTINE *running again.*

ALL (*on mic, singing*).
She said go
You can get there on your own
What is left here if you stay?
Cos it'll all come round again.

We switch back to PENNY *and* MARTIN *in the Cortina. The music fades to a crackle.*

EMILY (*on mic*). The radio crackles. Half-news. Half-static.

JIMMY (*on mic*). Penny winds down the window and lets in the scent of the hot summer night.

EMILY (*on mic*). They're turning right.

RICH appears. He's at the gig. The rest of the cast provide backing vocal 'aahs'.

RICH (*singing*).
We were seventeen,
Dancing to Tommy's guitar chords,
Now we're sailing on a boat,
Across the Norfolk Broads

A wild crowd of fans appear, dancing to RICH's song.

ALL. **You're the only one I need!**

RICH. Thank you, you've been a beautiful audience, have a great night!

ALL (*continuing to sing*). **You're the only one I need, yeah, only one I need.**

We see CHRISTINE, her hair blows in the wind.

ANNA and TESSA appear on a bench. ANNA leans in to kiss her.

TESSA. No, not here.

TESSA and ANNA run across the stage.

ANNA. Where are we going?

TESSA. I don't know – where do you want to go?

ANNA. My shoes are hurting!

TESSA. Then take them off!

We see MARTIN and PENNY in the car.

TESSA and ANNA run in front of MARTIN's car in slow motion.

ANTON appears smiling, full of joy, blowing glitter into the air.

We cut back to PENNY and MARTIN.

MEADOWS (*on mic*). Penny and Martin step out of the car.

EMILY (*on mic*). They zigzag up the gravelled path to Martin's front door.

We see TESSA *and* ANNA.

JIMMY (*on mic*). Tessa and Anna reach Tessa's battered front door. Tessa checks her front pocket, back pocket, jacket pocket.

TESSA. Fuck!

JIMMY. And before Anna knows it Tessa's off, up the drainpipe and through the bathroom window.

We see CHRISTINE.

BEN (*on mic*). Christine reaches the stained-glass window of the front door of her parents' semi-detached. Number 17. She fumbles to find her keys,

CHRISTINE. Argh!

BEN (*on mic*). – scrambles to make her way inside, then maybe she can breathe. Christine opens the door.

JIMMY (*on mic*). Martin opens the door.

BEN (*on mic*). Tessa opens the door.

12.

TESSA*'s house*.

ANNA *is overexcited*.

ANNA. Thanks again for inviting me tonight.

TESSA. Shhh.

ANNA. Sorry. I'm really glad I came. I nearly didn't come. I've never done anything like this before. You probably do this sort of stuff all the time.

TESSA. Shhh.

ANNA. I've never stayed out this late in my life. My parents are gonna kill me!

TESSA. Anna! Shh!

ANNA. Sorry. I haven't been up this late since the Moon Landing.

TESSA. I didn't watch it.

ANNA. Why not?

TESSA. I dunno. You've got all these white men in suits patting each other on the back. It's not really my thing.

ANNA. – You're the coolest person I've ever met in my life.

ANNA *and* TESSA *step away from each other.*

HELENA (*on mic*). Outside the toilets. A Britney Spears concert. Wembley Stadium. The year 2000.

NARRATORS (*on mic, like Britney Spears*). Oh babeh, babeh.

TESSA *sees* ANNA *through an imagined crowd.*

TESSA'S HEAD (*on mic*). It can't be, Anna, Anna Grant?

TESSA. It ain't exactly Lou Reed, is it?

ANNA'S HEAD (*on mic*). Tessa?

ANNA *turns.*

ANNA. Tessa!

TESSA. Anna.

ANNA. Oh my god! What are you doing here?

ANNA'S HEAD (*on mic*). Wow, she looks great.

ANNA. It's so good to see you. It's been…

TESSA. Way too long.

ANNA. Yeah.

TESSA. What are you doing at a Britney concert?

ANNA. It's my girlfriend's niece, she had to work late so I said I'd do the honours. She loves it 'Oops I Did It Again' and all that, she's obsessed.

TESSA. My kids are the same.

ANNA. Kids?

ANNA'S HEAD (*on mic*). Kids?

TESSA. Yeah, two of them.

ANNA. Wow.

ANNA'S HEAD (*on mic*). Kids?

ANNA. That's great.

TESSA. David is eleven – he's smart as anything, and Ziggy, she's nine, she's so creative…

ANNA. Ziggy?

TESSA. Yeah.

ANNA. That's pretty…

ANNA'S HEAD (*on mic*). Pretentious.

TESSA. It seemed like a good idea at the time. But now she hates me for it, calls herself Sarah instead.

ANNA'S HEAD (*on mic*). Not surprised.

ANNA. So tell me about you. Are you seeing anyone?

TESSA. Yeah… James and I have been together for about twelve years now.

ANNA Okay, right.

ANNA'S HEAD (*on mic*). James? A man? Twelve years?

TESSA. Anna?

TESSA'S HEAD. Why is she being so odd?

TESSA. What is it?

ANNA. Oh god. Sorry. It's just… It's just strange that you would, that you would want to –

ANNA'S HEAD (*on mic*). James?

ANNA. It's nothing.

TESSA. Anna…

TESSA'S HEAD (*on mic*). Don't talk to me like that.

ANNA. It just changes something for me that's all.

ANNA'S HEAD (*on mic*). I'm being unfair, and I know that, I'm being this fucking narrow-minded arsehole. I'm sorry. I just don't think –

ANNA. You're with a man?

TESSA. You realise that's really unfair.

ANNA. I know.

TESSA. Okay.

ANNA. Okay.

TESSA. Right

ANNA. Ziggy…?

TESSA. Yeah.

ANNA. That's really pretentious.

TESSA. Yeah I know.

    Pause.

HELENA (*on mic*). Anna and Tessa really look at each other.

ANNA. I'll see you.

TESSA. See you.

ANNA (*back in 1972*). You're the coolest person I've ever met in my life.

TESSA. Shut up.

    TESSA *and* ANNA *kiss.*

13.

MARTIN*'s flat.*

PENNY *and* MARTIN *are reading poetry, turning pages delicately and sensually.*

PENNY. These are really good… The onomatopoeias, just… wow…

MARTIN. I'm not actually reading anything.

PENNY. Yeah neither am I, so…

They drop the books. They kiss passionately. PENNY *pulls away.*

Can you just give me a second?

PENNY *walks to one corner.*

BEN (*on mic*). Penny goes to the bathroom.

MARTIN. That's a cupboard.

PENNY (*on mic*). Right okay, got you.

PENNY *walks to the other corner. In the bathroom,* PENNY *screams and jumps with joy.* LADY CHATTERLEY *enters.*

LADY CHATTERLEY. Penny.

PENNY. Lady Chatterley!?

LADY CHATTERLEY. I hereby dub you Penny, Queen of the Realm of Sex. You know what to do.

PENNY *and* LADY CHATTERLEY *high-five.* PENNY *exits the bathroom.*

She marches over to MARTIN *and kisses him.*

MARTIN *touches* PENNY*'s breast.*

MARTIN. Sorry.

PENNY. You're welcome. No! I mean, sorry. No, I mean that felt good, that felt really good.

MARTIN. Good. Okay. Good.

They kiss again. MARTIN *pulls away.*

Sorry I don't have any…

PENNY. It's okay, I'm on the –

MARTIN. Great. Right. Okay then.

They kiss. They turn away from each other. They scream.

14.

ANTON*'s bedroom.* ANTON *stands, looking at himself in the mirror.*

KERRY (*on mic*). This is Anthony. His parents call him Anthony. His friends call him Tony. He calls himself Anton. Anton sees in his reflection the person he wants to be and in that moment decides to face the world. He goes to the door.

ANTON *moves to leave.*

He is no longer afraid.

ENGLAND (*on mic*). But then he stops himself.

ANTON *stops.*

Anton knows nothing good can come from this. He thinks to himself what am I doing here? What would my father think? He goes to get his clothes back on.

KERRY (*on mic*). And then he thinks, it's now or never to face this brave new world where he will be accepted for who he wants to be and what he wants to wear.

ENGLAND (*on mic*). But he sees his father's face reflected back at him, that look of disappointment, the disgust, 'I never want to see you again. People are not ready for that and they never will be.'

KERRY (*on mic*). It's 1972. People are ready. Or would you rather he stayed in his room and hung himself?

ENGLAND (*on mic*). But he still feels trapped. He's trapped in his own space.

HELENA *enters* ANTON*'s bedroom.*

HELENA (*on mic. To* ENGLAND). Anton could go outside. In fact I think it would be better if he did go outside / because then he wouldn't just be stuck in his room where no one could accept him anyway.

KERRY (*on mic*). / Anton is proud of who he is.

BEN (*on mic*). – His parents' generation are still quite intolerant. We don't wanna alienate them. So maybe we just take it in baby steps.

The NARRATORS *enter the space.* ANTON *looks bewildered.*

MEADOWS (*on mic*). He can't just run off into the night and join the love brigade –

KERRY (*on mic*). Yes he can, his parents are proud of who he is.

The arguing becomes an incomprehensible mass of voices. ANTON *brings a microphone into the space and bangs it. High-pitched feedback.*

The NARRATORS *become silent.*

The NARRATORS *leave.*

ANTON *becomes* ANTON'S DAD. *For the rest of the scene,* ANTON *switches between* ANTON *and* ANTON'S DAD.

ANTON'S DAD. Anthony?
Anthony, can I come in a sec?
I just wanna have a chat, lad.

ANTON'S DAD *pauses.*

ANTON *stands in front of the mirror.*

Alright, I'll say my piece out here. Your mother and I have been worried about you, son. You've not been eating properly, you've barely said a word in weeks. What is it, lad? Trouble at school?

ANTON'S DAD *pauses.*

ANTON *stands, unable to move.*

Your mother's noticed a few of her things have gone missing.

ANTON *looks down at his clothes.*

You're not in the doghouse, son, far from it.

Anthony?

Pause.

Dinner's on the table in ten.

I'm leaving now.

ANTON'S DAD *leaves.*

ANTON *looks at himself in the mirror and exhales.*

15.

MARTIN *dances sensually for* PENNY.

TESSA *dances in the same way for* ANNA.

MARTIN, PENNY, TESSA *and* ANNA *pull off their partner's and their own clothes to reveal swimming costumes. They put on goggles.*

Swelling, overwhelming music.

They dive in.

RICH *and* CHRISTINE *appear across the stage from each other.*

They shout to reach each other over the music.

RICH. What the hell –

CHRISTINE. I want to

RICH. Is going on?

CHRISTINE. I want to do it

RICH. Where have you

CHRISTINE. for you and

RICH. been?

CHRISTINE. and us and

RICH. Why weren't you

CHRISTINE. me

RICH. at my gig.

CHRISTINE. Every time I think of

RICH. I was waiting

CHRISTINE. actually doing it

RICH. absolutely ages.

CHRISTINE. it makes me want

RICH. Have you been

CHRISTINE. to cry

RICH. at home

CHRISTINE. I'm so angry

RICH. preparing candles

CHRISTINE. at myself because

RICH. or something like that

CHRISTINE. I was fucking convinced.

RICH. because I don't want

CHRISTINE. I didn't lie

RICH. any of that

CHRISTINE. about it and

RICH. I just want

CHRISTINE. I was supposed to be

RICH. You

CHRISTINE. important

RICH. why can't you get that?

CHRISTINE. to you

RICH. is this about someone else

CHRISTINE. I can't

RICH. Or are you just

CHRISTINE. Do that

RICH. freaking out

CHRISTINE. I love you

RICH. I don't want to mess

CHRISTINE. I can't

RICH. This up, this means

CHRISTINE. do that.

RICH. A lot to me

CHRISTINE. I love you, I can't do that.

> RICH *and* CHRISTINE *disappear.*

> PENNY, MARTIN, ANNA *and* TESSA *sprint across the stage as the music swells.*

> ANTON *appears androgynous, angelic.* ANTON *adopts various 'beautiful' poses.*

> ANNA, MARTIN *and* TESSA *all have a moment of release.*

> *The couples sink to the floor, gabbling.*

> ANTON *lowers a mic to each of their mouths.*

16.

A dark stage.

TESSA, ANNA, MARTIN *and* PENNY *are lying on the floor, panting.*

We hear TESSA *and* ANNA*'s voices in the dark.*

TESSA (*on mic*). So…

ANNA (*on mic*). So…

TESSA (*on mic*). I can hear your heart beating.

ANNA (*on mic*). Yeah it does that. I've got this extra beat. Can you hear it?

TESSA (*on mic*). Yeah. I've got this thing when I fall asleep. It's a twitch, that goes from my head, through my body. Sorry if I twitch.

ANNA (*on mic*). Sorry if I snore.

17.

We hear MARTIN *and* PENNY*'s voices in the dark. Heavy breathing.*

PENNY (*on mic*). I've wanted to do that for so long.

MARTIN (*on mic*). Me too.

PENNY (*on mic*). So, I haven't quite got there yet.

MARTIN (*on mic*). Sorry, I thought you'd…

PENNY (*on mic*). No. It was so good. But I don't orgasm that way. I know what works though. You just have to use your tongue.

MARTIN (*on mic*). I've never done that before.

PENNY (*on mic*). Oh, it's alright. I can guide you through it.

MARTIN (*on mic*). No, I don't want to.

PENNY (*on mic*). What?

MARTIN (*on mic*). I don't want to, Penny.

PENNY (*on mic*). But your lessons, what you teach…

MARTIN (*on mic*). I don't teach this.

PENNY (*on mic*). But I don't understand, all your lessons, all those people you introduced me to, all your theories…

MARTIN (*on mic*). They're just theories.

PENNY (*on mic*). Oh.

18.

RICH *and* CHRISTINE *enter.*

RICH. I lit some candles for you.

CHRISTINE. Yeah you did.

RICH. Christine, they're not supposed to put any pressure… We don't have to… I can wait.

CHRISTINE. I don't know how long I'm going to be. I don't want to make you wait that long.

RICH. It's fine. I just wanted to create a magical atmosphere, but we don't need to have sex for it to be magical, we can just… hold hands. Can we do that? Can we hold hands?

CHRISTINE. Yeah, we can do that.

CHRISTINE *and* RICH *hold hands and sit in the row of chairs from the show's opening.*

19.

PENNY *gets up from her position on the floor and looks for her clothes. During her text,* TESSA, ANNA *and* MARTIN *rise from the floor and sit on the row of seats from the show's opening while* PENNY *continues to search.*

PENNY (*on mic*). To the class of '72:

To quote the musical *Hair* –

'Harmony and understanding, sympathy and trust abounding.' Yes. I have great faith in that.

In the future, language will be redesigned to oppress no one. We will communicate with truth and utter honesty. Women will talk and do as much as men with as much volume. The world will be ruled by family, a global union – of brothers and sisters. Everyone will be cared for and respected.

In the future, I do genuinely believe that things will be better. Women will be able to be angry and sad and not be called crazy or hysterical. And men will be vulnerable and be thought the better for it.

In the future, colourful clothes will be plucked from genderless shelves at will. And lovers will fuck with love. The world will spin off into an orgy of peace and love and –

20.

ANTON (*on mic*). – And Penny came second in the run for Union President.

And she found a boyfriend called John and another called Terry and then she married her boyfriend called Tim. And they had a daughter called Rose and they lived in Acton, and on Saturdays they would watch *Take Me Out* and talk about how outrageous it all was and reminisce about the simple days of *Blind Date*.

PENNY *leaves*.

And Penny seldom thought of Martin and Martin often thought of her.

MARTIN *leaves*.

And Tessa would take great joy in showing her children photographs of herself when she was young.

TESSA *leaves*.

And her and Anna would meet again at a Britney Spears concert and would feel a gulf between them.

ANNA *leaves*.

And Germaine Greer appeared on *Big Brother* and they both felt a sense of personal betrayal.

And Rich would soon give up his dreams of rockstardom to become an electrician. And years later he would contact Christine via Friends Reunited telling her that he still thought of her often and that he had never loved another woman as much as her.

RICH *leaves*.

And Christine would stare at the screen for a very long time, all the while twisting the ring on her finger.

CHRISTINE *leaves*.

And Tommy, the guitarist from the band, who loved Hatty the barmaid from The Cross Club would finally touch her naked body on the dark dance floor after the club had closed.

MUSICIAN *leaves*.

ANTON *moves into the centre*.

And Anna's mum would have a brief, passionate affair with her next-door neighbour, and Anna's dad would never know and he would rarely desire his wife.

And Michael, the drummer, would move to America and change his name to Mikey. And he would continue to love Christine.

And George, the boy with the petition, would make love to three men after a Fleetwood Mac concert and would later blame his behaviour on being wasted.

And Susan, who liked to be spanked, would orgasm loudly on a balcony one Sunday morning in September.

And Tariq, who liked to have his toes sucked, would tell his wife of seven years of his secret desire and she would smile gently and take off his shoes.

And Roberta would pine for someone, anyone to cure her of her loneliness and it would hurt her so deeply that she would jump from a church spire one cold afternoon in March.

And Dale and Charlie, two childhood friends would ignore the warnings of their parents and continue to kiss and touch and fuck.

And so on, and so forth, and all these little earthquakes gradually faded away and new earthquakes came to take their place.

And Anton opened his door and he went downstairs and he ate dinner with his parents and he told them about his day and he asked them about their day and…

Blackout.

A Nick Hern Book

1972: The Future of Sex first published in Great Britain in 2019 as a paperback original by Nick Hern Books Limited, The Glasshouse, 49a Goldhawk Road, London W12 8QP, in association with The Wardrobe Ensemble

1972: The Future of Sex copyright © 2019 The Wardrobe Ensemble

The Wardrobe Ensemble have asserted their moral right to be identified as the authors of this work

Cover image: © Louie Isaaman-Jones

Designed and typeset by Nick Hern Books, London
Printed in the UK by Mimeo Ltd, Huntingdon, Cambridgeshire PE29 6XX

A CIP catalogue record for this book is available from the British Library

ISBN 978 1 84842 847 8

Woodland
CARBON
www.woodlandcarbon.co.uk
NICK HERN BOOKS
Printed on Carbon Captured paper

www.nickhernbooks.co.uk

 facebook.com/nickhernbooks

 twitter.com/nickhernbooks